All Kinds of Castles

by Isabel Thomas

Stone Castles

What do you picture when you think about castles? You might picture something like this.

Lots of castles are made from strong stone. Stone castles could protect people from **sieges** and battles. Many old stone castles are still standing!

Not all castles are made of stone. Have you ever seen a castle made of these things?

wood

brick

snow

glass

Let's find out where you can see these castles!

Wooden Castles

The very first castles were made from wood. Wood comes from trees. It is easy to transport and cut into shapes.

However, wood burns or rots when it gets wet. Wooden castles did not last very long.

This wooden castle has been **reconstructed**.

Mud Castles

This giant castle in Iran is made from adobe.

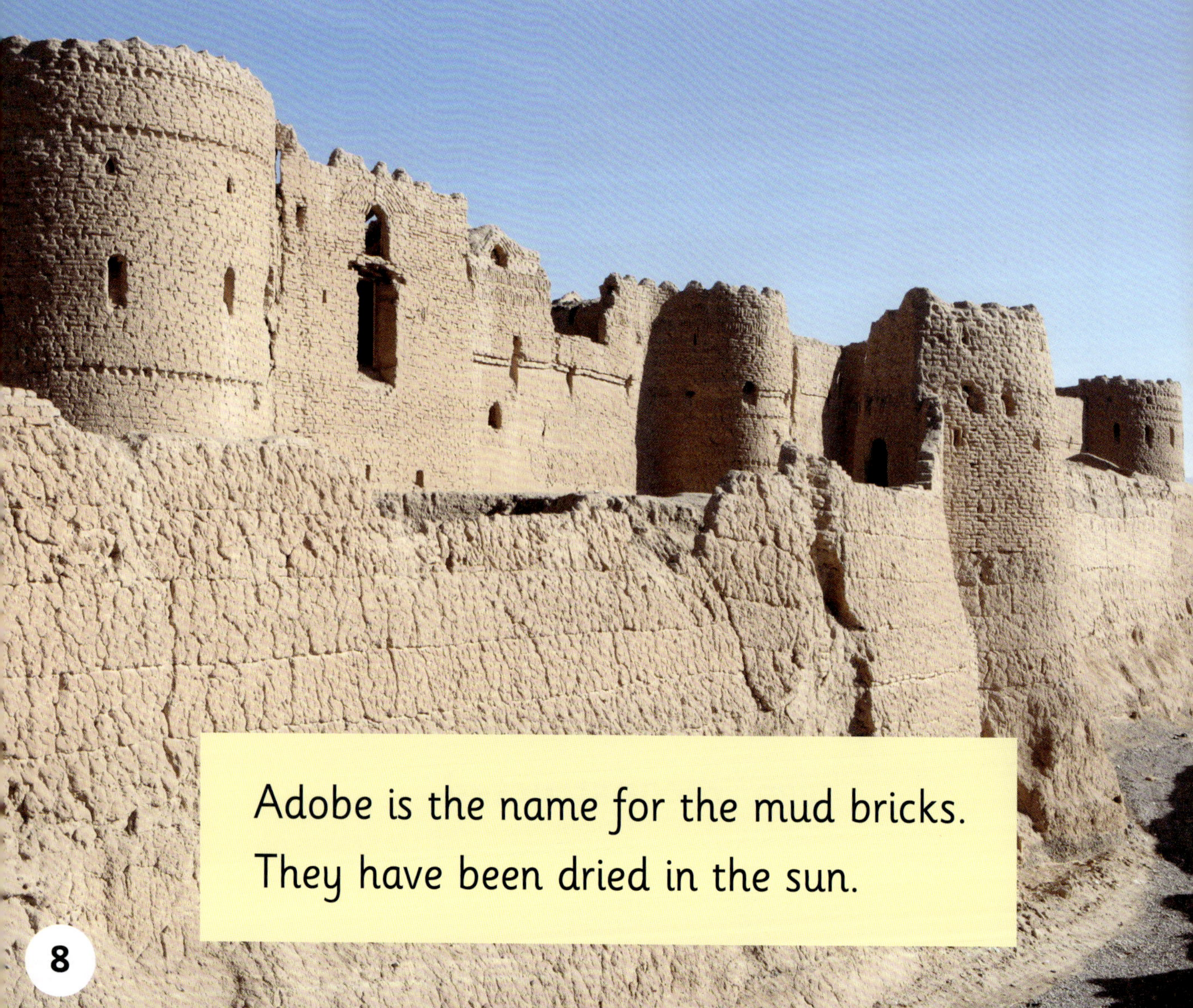

Adobe is the name for the mud bricks. They have been dried in the sun.

Mud bricks do not burn or rot like wood. These adobe castles are over 1000 years old!

Most adobe castles are in dry parts of the world. That's because rain can weaken mud bricks.

Brick Castles

This castle in Poland is made of clay bricks. They won't budge in a rainstorm.

Clay bricks are baked in a hot **kiln**. This makes them stronger.

Frozen Castles

This frozen castle is in China. It is made from giant blocks of snow. People travel by sledge to visit it.

This frozen castle sits on a lake in Canada.
It looks magical as it glistens in the sun.
Inside, it is colder than a fridge!

Castles in Nature

Some people cut hedges into the shape of castles. What a strange-looking castle!

This castle is for children to play in. It is in the trees. Try imagining you are playing here. If you listen, you can hear birds tweeting!

Fragile Castles

Some castles are far too small for people to go inside. They are made to look at! This glass castle is very **fragile**.

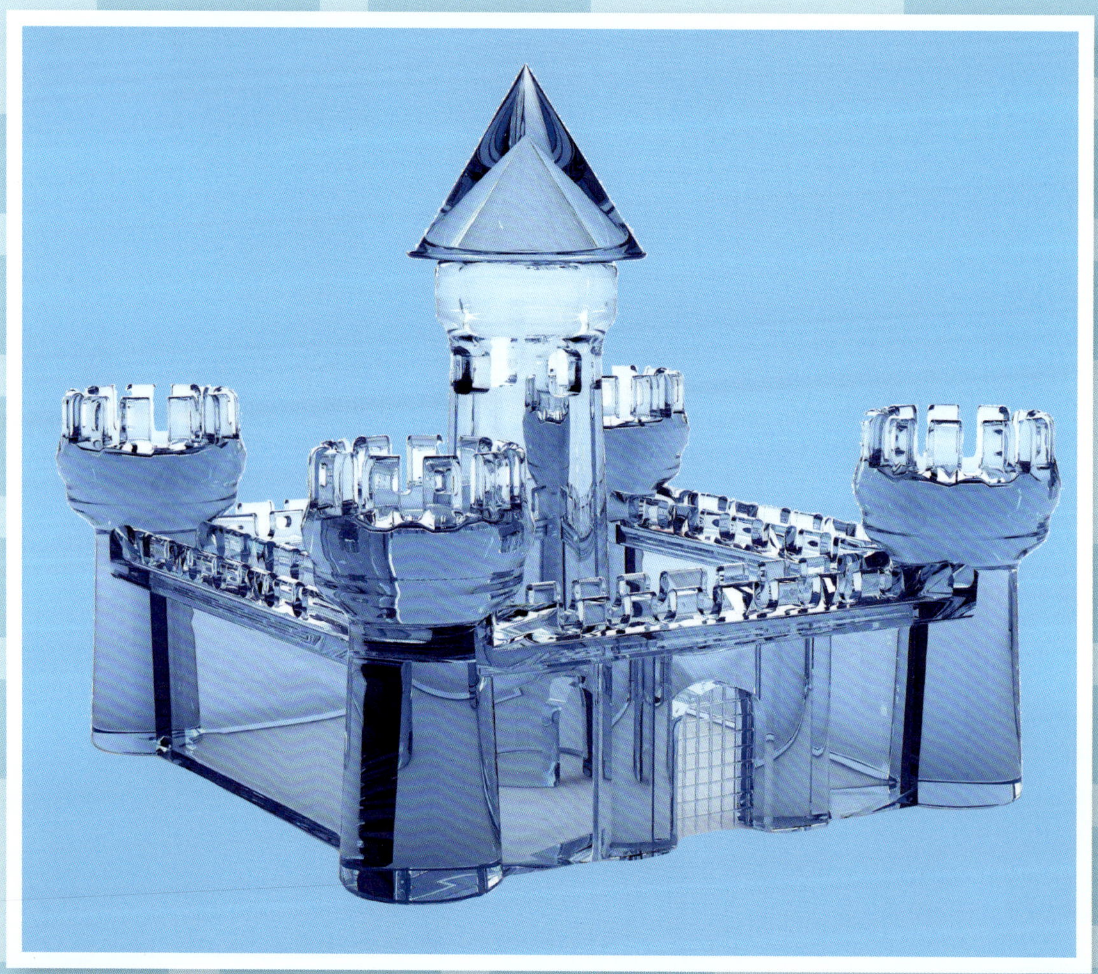

Even paper can be made into a castle! This is a model of a large castle in Germany.

the original castle

Sandcastles

Have you ever made a sandcastle? You must be very gentle when you make it. Just one nudge can topple the sandcastle!

People challenge themselves to make bigger and better sandcastles. If you were the **judge**, which castle would you pick?

Toy Castles

You don't have to make a castle at the beach. Here are two things you could use at home.

boxes

plastic bricks

Challenge yourself! Can you make a castle at home? It could be small or large!

This huge castle is made from plastic bricks.

Cake Castles!

You can even make a castle from food! This is a cake castle.

Invite some friends to help you eat your cake castle.

Glossary

fragile: easy to break

judge: someone who picks the winner

kiln: an oven for baking clay to make it hard

reconstructed: something which is made again

sieges: when people surround places to take control of them

Index